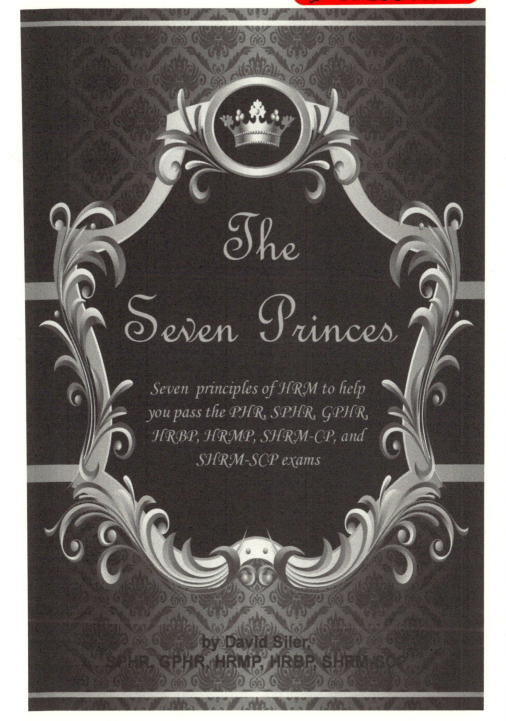

# The

# Seven Princes

*Seven principles of HRM to help you pass the PHR, SPHR, GPHR, HRBP, HRMP, SHRM-CP, and SHRM-SCP exams*

by David Siler,
SPHR, GPHR, HRMP, HRBP, SHRM-SCP

ISBN 978-1-939536-91-4

Distinctive Human Resources, Inc.
221 N. Horner Blvd.
Sanford, NC 27330

# Foreword

I designed the concept of The Seven Princes to help certification candidates pass the: SPHR, PHR, GPHR, HRMP, HRBP, SHRM-SCP and SHRM-CP exams. Too many candidates struggle with the "strategic" questions on these tests. These soft, ambiguous, vague, and fuzzy questions drive many test-takers mad. With this guidebook, I hope to change that.

While these seven HRM principles will aid you on your quest towards certification, they are universally applied to almost any situation an HR professional may encounter. I am convinced that if learned well, these seven fundamental principles of HRM will set the modern and progressive practitioner on a path to becoming an HR legend. With their use, you may well become a trusted and respected member of the strategic leadership team. But, I do not care about that. My only goal is seeing you earn your letters. So, learn your lessons well. Go get 'em, Tiger!

*David Siler*, SPHR, GPHR, HRMP, HRBP, SHRM-SCP

# Contents

# The Seven Princes

(Seven key principles of HRM, essential for passing the HR certification exams)
by
David Siler, SPHR, GPHR, HRMP, HRBP

After 20 years of designing, creating and teaching preparation programs for HR certification exams, I have learned some "do's" and "don'ts" for passing these exams on the first try. These lessons did not come easily. They were developed from trial and error by working with thousands of candidates. Many of these  lessons fly in the face of conventional wisdom.

The reason almost half of the Certificants fail their exam on the first try is they do not alter their preparations process for the type test they encounter. And what's mind boggling to me, despite my experience and coaching, many of my candidates will simply be too stubborn or too engrained in study-habit ideology to be able to alter their preparation approaches. That's OK, you can do it your way and possibly retake the exam by ignoring my advice and dropping another $1,000+/- and investing a lot more of your personal time in preparations, or you can follow the guidelines I will lay out for you in this booklet that will enhance the probability of passing on the first attempt. So, are you going to be stubborn or smart?

To successfully achieve the goal of earning your credentials, you will have to unlearn many of the lessons and study habits that aided you back when you were at a tender young age. You will need to rethink your strategies and approaches for preparing for these nasty and demanding exams.

As I have said, it is often prohibitively costly in both time and money to not get it right the first time. To give yourself the best possible chance, prepare yourself to fundamentally change the way you have always approached the educational testing process. If you cannot accomplish this transformation, failure is a strong possibility.

But never fear, this guidebook is here to give you the insights you will need for success. Make no mistake, passing these exams is an ordeal of epic proportions and any advantage you can get will move you one step closer to your goal. So, listen up and pay attention.

First, I want to talk about the "Don'ts." For example, the most important difference between the HR certification exams and the exams you took in High School and at University is that you can't memorize your way to a successful outcome.

In school, the teacher handed out the text books and you were told to study each chapter thoroughly. Then, you took a test and hopefully scored well since the questions came directly from that book. Often, it was possible to get 80-90%+/- of the questions correct with that preparatory approach. If you were really clever and studied really hard, perhaps 100%. Not so with the HR certification exams. If you can score 70% or better on these exams, you are in the elite of the HR intelligentsia. Plus, you have no life since you study so much and we all feel sorry for you.

Let me say this plainly, many of the test questions you will be challenged with do not come out of anybody's study manual. Instead, they come from application of theory. They come from experience and understanding. They come from practitioners who know there are many ways to look at the same situation. More on this later.

By now, you are one page into this book and you are already doubting whether it contains the truth. I am telling you to abandon the system you used to successfully pull good grades in High School and College. I am telling you not to count on gleaning the proper and needed information from printed materials by memorizing the content. If that is what you have heard so far, then excellent, because yes, that is exactly what I am saying.

I can hear you now saying, "but, but, but... that is the way we were trained from an early age to learn a topic!" Yeah, yeah, yeah, I get it, I know how you were trained. I was trained that way too. But it will not work as well for these certification exams.

Don't get me wrong, there is a certain amount of study and memorization you will have to accomplish, but it is relatively minor in regards to the scope of the profession. With literally thousands of potential topics that could appear on your test, memorizing all of that material is practically an impossibility.

So, focusing on the details and missing the overall purpose of the subject is one of the most common prep mistakes I see candidates making. Let me say again, drilling too far down in the weeds, clouds the true purpose of the HR topic. Your goal, young Padawan, is to seek enlightenment and understanding. Not to memorize a bunch of useless garbage.

Too Zen for you?

Let's put it this way, I advise my candidates to "skim" my study manual. I do not want them to reach a state of analysis paralysis in studying each item until the words come off the page of the guidebook. I admonish them over and over to lightly learn the topics, but more importantly, learn to apply them to the situations and scenarios that appear on the exam. However, they often cannot stop themselves from deeply studying dates, names of theorists, details of employment laws, and the minutiae of the HR field. This approach accomplishes very little, is a great waste of time and effort, and hinders their focus on reaching a state of application-focused understanding. Which is what I want for them... not to mention it is required to pass the exams.

You see, "understanding" the material is the goal. Knowing how to apply it. Identifying the advantages and disadvantages. Understanding the timing of application. Realizing the downstream effect a new policy will have on morale. Playing corporate politics. Making the right choice when an ethical conflict arises. Being able to organize and lay out the plan of work for a new HR initiative while satisfying the goals of the operations department.

Very little of the things I have mentioned comes from a book but all of these skill sets are required on the HR certification exams.

Without them, you will have a difficult time earning your credentials. Embrace them, your path to entering the HR Hall of Fame is likely.

So, what is our plan? If you can steal a little time away from studying and memorizing to learn a few basic principles of Human Resource Management (HRM), I can help you answer perhaps dozens of questions on the certification tests. I have spent a lot of time identifying the basic HRM concepts that show up again and again on the exam.

These seven basic rules of HRM are applicable to multiple scenarios and situations that you probably will encounter on the exams. Learning them may be the most efficient use of your time in all of your preparation efforts since they have such widespread application. Further, playing with the practice questions I will throw at you will get you to apply and develop your reasoning skills... which you are going to need, big time!

Allow me to introduce you to the seven essential principles of HRM that I call, "The Seven Princes." To the uninitiated, these should probably be called, "The Seven Devils."

1. Needs analysis
2. Top management commitment
3. Operational support
4. Critical thinking skills
5. Most valuable assets
6. Communication
7. Employee participation

These seven principles of HRM are the keys to unlocking the mysteries of passing the HR exams and to reducing the adversity of the testing process. By understanding and applying these values, multiple questions will prove solvable. Without understanding and embracing these doctrines, many questions will look like they are written in a foreign language.

So you can better comprehend what I am describing, take a look at the below sample question and circle your selection as to the correct answer.

<u>Sample Question 1:</u>
The primary goal of any employee development initiative is to produce:
   A.  Greater employee satisfaction and engagement
   B.  A sustainable record of employee KSA's
   C.  Measurable results towards productivity
   D.  Deeper talent for future needs

*The answer is at the end of this section.* Yeah, yeah, it's OK, go ahead and jump forward to see if you got it right. If you did, lucky you. If you didn't, no worries, the Seven Princes will help you out on these head scratchers. The next seven chapters are devoted to providing you the basic information needed to understand and apply the Seven Princes. After each section, you will be asked to use these lessons to answer a series of practice questions that are representative of the HR certification exams. Pay attention, learn these lessons well and fear not the evil certification monster for you will be a beast slayer.

Answer to Question 1:
"C" is the best answer as it helps provide operational support - Prince #3.
Much of the resources allocated to training are wasted. That is, there are no
measurable or obvious positive results in terms of better employee
contributions or productivity for immediate organizational needs. While the
other answer options have value, improving productivity is the core business
goal. Training initiatives must be planned and linked properly towards the
business and operational objectives. Otherwise, why bother?

# Prince #1 - Needs Assessment

## (Failing to plan is planning to fail)

Which comes first, the chicken or the egg? To determine the best answer on your certification exam, first study the situation to determine which is the higher priority based on organizational requirements. Organizations have to determine the "need" for either the chicken or the egg. The one with the greatest "need" is the one that comes first. Plain and simple!

Without identifying the need, candidates have a reduced chance of guessing correctly. Different organizations and different departments within those organizations will have different needs and therefore, different priorities. Thus, some will go with the egg and others the chicken.

OK, enough of the clever analogy. Time to get serious.

The "needs analysis" is usually the first step taken when there is any form of change that must occur in the workplace. A needs analysis is an activity utilized to plan effectively, indentify priorities, make decisions, and solve problems. It's application is critical for any new initiative to have any hope for success. Without conducting one, mistakes will be made, time will be wasted, dollars will be pointlessly spent, and people will be fired for being lame brains.

*The moral of this story; step back, slow down, and study the situation prior to committing company resources when a change is mandated. In other words, study first, act secondly. The identification of the "need" is the first step in a uniform approach to solving any organization issue. Saying again, the "need" is the FIRST step in any problem solving process.*

Conducting a needs assessment, sometimes called a "gap analysis," is relatively simple. It is the difference between the actual level of job performance and the expected level of job performance. It will help identify whether it is an organizational issue, a problem with employee performance, or a task issue. Or, it may not be a problem at all and is simply a new initiative being launched due to market demands. Regardless, an effective needs analysis, at the beginning of the process, will help direct company resources to areas of greatest demand.

In summary, the purpose of this manual is to aid in the preparations for the HR certification exams and not in the "how to" conduct a needs assessment. Therefore, the one and only point being made is to conduct a needs analysis FIRST... always, always, always!

Now, it is time to test your skills in applying this lesson. Remember, no matter how sexy some of the other answer options look, "needs analysis" comes first... unless you are a lame brain. And, even when you get the answers correct on these practice questions, study the explanations until they become second nature. They are loaded with informative tidbits that will aid in your comprehension, understanding and application of the concepts. Practice quizzes are your most powerful learning and preparation tool. Use them!

# Practice Quiz (Prince #1):

1. At which stage should a training "needs analysis" be conducted?
   A. After top management has committed support
   B. After the problems have been identified
   C. After resources have been allocated
   D. Prior to any other action

2. For greatest effectiveness, what is the first step in creating a new training program?
   A. Identifying the instructor
   B. Quantifying the costs
   C. Ascertaining organizational requirements
   D. Categorizing methods for evaluating results

3. To be most effective, what is the first step the Training Manager should take when creating a new instructional program?
   A. Gain top management commitment
   B. Define organizational and individual requirements
   C. Align the program goals with business objectives
   D. Ensure employee engagement is included in the process

4. Before designing a new performance management system, the HR manager should begin the process by:
   A. Identifying the goals of the new initiative
   B. Assigning staff members to the implementation team
   C. Seeking a top-management champion
   D. Developing and gathering anticipated resources

5. What is the primary purpose for conducting a "needs analysis?"
   A. To provide quantifiable data to gain top management commitment
   B. To study success factors for organizational transitions
   C. To direct resources to areas of greatest demand
   D. It forms the foundation for manpower forecasting

## Answers and explanations:

1    D- Prince #1 postulates that the purpose of a training needs assessment is to identify performance requirements and the knowledge, skills, and abilities (KSA's) needed by an agency's workforce to achieve the requirements. This should happen prior to any other steps being taken in the process. The needs analysis should be conducted first to aid in obtaining top management commitment, identifying the source of the problems, and to focus the allocation of resources to the area's most in need.

2    C - Prince #1 says the purpose of a training needs assessment is to identify performance requirements and the knowledge, skills, and abilities needed by an agency's workforce to achieve the requirements. The difference between the actual level of job performance and the expected level of job performance indicates a need for training. The identification of the organizational requirements is the first step in a uniform method of instructional design.

3    B - Prince #1 requires the identification of training needs to be the first step in a uniform method of instructional design. A successful training needs analysis will identify those who need training and what kind of training is needed. It is counter-productive to offer training to individuals who do not need it or to offer the wrong kind of training. A Training Needs Analysis helps to put the training resources to good use.

4    A - Per the ADDIE model, the first step in any process is to conduct a needs analysis - Prince #1. The needs analysis occurs directly before the design stage begins. In this case, determining the goals of the project is a necessary component of the organizational needs assessment.

5    C - Prince #1 theorizes an effective needs assessment will efficiently direct organizational resources to areas of greatest demand. The assessment should address resources needed to fulfill the firm's mission, improve productivity, and provide quality products and services in the most efficient manner possible.

# Prince #2 - Top Management Commitment

## (If Mama's not happy, nobody's happy)

Have you ever felt alone, exposed, or hung-out-to dry? Of course you have, and without top management supporting your position, you will again. Thus, it is imperative, critical, vital, essential, important, fundamental, and necessary that top management commits to support any new HR endeavor before it begins. Without their backing, you are quite possibly doomed to a humiliating and soul-crushing defeat... even when you are right.

The reality of the situation is inescapable. Without top management buy-in, employees and peers will never fully support any new enterprise. Most employees break their backs to please their bosses, so if they see a new HR program unsupported, they will abandon and ignore it no matter how worthwhile the cause.

*Therefore, your lesson this time, young grasshopper, always seek and obtain top management support prior to launching any new proposal.*

"Wait, wait, wait," you say. I thought we were to first execute Prince #1 and conduct the needs analysis? That is absolutely correct. However, once you have the results of the needs analysis, you will use that information to help sell top management on the necessity of the new proposition. Therefore, once the needs analysis proves your position, the next step is to pitch the new scheme to potential management champions. If they turn down the request, throw the plan in the garbage.

If management expresses verbal support but hedges on providing resources, again, throw the project in the garbage. Employees are clever and will see right through lip-service levels of support. Also, employees are busy and their time is limited. They will help those projects that are getting support and attention from their bosses. They will discount those without backing and will laugh at your efforts to tilt windmills.

If top management throws their support to a project, it must be seen throughout the organization and not just in the conference room. Their commitment must be unqualified, loud, very apparent, and visual. They must be living, breathing, role models. Further, they must continue to support it throughout the life of the program. Both during implementation and throughout system operation. Without their active commitment, the application will run out of energy and die a painful (for you) death.

The type of support management should provide includes the resources necessary to accomplish the new endeavor that includes: personnel, funding, time, materials, etc.

In conclusion, it is clear that without top management buy-in, it is a tactical error to try and continue a project no matter its strategic merits. Therefore, on the HR exams, when asked what is "most essential" when launching any new initiative, choose "management commitment," if that option is provided.

OK, time to put the lesson to practice. Here are a few questions where the best answer will involve "top management support."

# Practice Quiz (Prince #2):

1.  What is the MOST important requirement for the HR Director to accomplish when proposing a new and innovative performance management system?
    A.  Obtain top management commitment·
    B.  Obtain operational financing
    C.  Plan system implementation
    D.  Develop metrics for system monitoring

2.  Prior to committing resources to a new HR proposal, the HR Director should first seek support from:
    A.  Those people opposing the proposal
    B.  Non-exempt employees
    C.  The executive team✓
    D.  The HR staff

3.  Which has the most strategic value for the HR department to obtain when launching a new organizational diversity initiative?
    A.  Training budget
    B.  Management support▪
    C.  Benchmark data
    D.  Acceptance by minority employees

4.  Conventional wisdom finds the most critical element to ensure success of an original and introductory undertaking is the:
    A.  Skill of the players involved
    B.  Strategic importance of the project
    C.  Cost benefit implications
    D.  Commitment and support of top management·

5.  Which is the MOST important prerequisite for the HR Manager when engaging operational managers to provide funding and participants for a new training initiative?
    A.  Defining requirements and preparing the presentation
    B.  Analyzing previous initiatives
    C.  Developing the budget and selecting participants
    D.  Presenting the requirements and securing commitment ·

## Answers and explanations:

1   A - Prince #2 claims that without top management support and commitment, the proposal is a waste of time. The HR Manager MUST obtain management's support or abandon the initiative.

2   C - Prince #2 requires the HR Director to obtain consent and support from the executive team. Failure to obtain their unqualified agreement, the HR Director should abandon this initiative.

3   B - Prince #2 postulates that management support is essential for any new initiative to succeed. Without it, the HR department should not go forward with this program. Always go with "Top management commitment" on any question you see on your certification exam that asks, "What's most important?"

4   D - Prince #2 postulates that management support is essential for any new initiative to succeed. Without it, the organization should not go forward with this undertaking.

5   D - Prince #2 theorizes that presenting the plan and securing support and commitment is the most important of the elements presented since without these the initiative will fail.

# Prince #3 - Operational Support

# (If you're not aligned, you're behind)

The term, "strategic business partner," gets thrown around a lot in HR circles. Often misapplied and misunderstood. In reality, it is not that complicated of a concept.

To earn the title of strategic business partner, HR practitioners must base all people decisions on the support of the business plan. To accomplish this, they must become more business savvy. If so, they will have a better shot at gaining a seat at the strategic planning table and be viewed as a valued and contributing member of the senior team.

Being invited to the strategy planning table is the goal. Not just attending in order to take care of dinner reservations and the caterer. Being viewed as an active and integrated partner is an honor that must be earned... and valued, once achieved.

To reach this goal, HR must align all its actions towards the accomplishment of the defined business objectives. Further, should HR prove to be competent and contributory to the commercial agenda, HR will be involved in creating and setting, not just following, corporate directives.

*Therefore, Prince #3 identifies as a core HRM principle, that organizational effectiveness begins with the alignment of an organization's workforce and human resource capabilities with the business objectives. This includes coordinating all aspects related to employee talent and performance to the accomplishment of the strategic business plan.*

Organizations simply cannot be effective without this alignment. An organization's ultimate success is a direct function of HR alignment.

Too long, HR has been viewed as an independent and rogue agency. Overly concerned with ice cream socials, planning holiday parties, or enforcing archaic and obsolete rules and regulations. Not an important team member that collaborates and assists on critical company projects. HR needs to keep its eye on the prize, providing actions and activities that will assist in carrying out the core production or service ventures.

Everything HR does must have a business justification and have the potential to positively impact the bottom-line. HR does not offer safety programs because of our love for our fellow man. We do not offer wellness programs because of our concern for the health and well-being of our colleagues. We do not offer Employee Assistance Programs (EAPs) to ease the personal burdens of workers because we care. Instead, we want our employees healthy, fit, and focused to be able to contribute to organizational welfare. We want employees on the job and not absent. We want them attentive and not distracted by family issues. We want them to make serious contributions. Which usually occurs when they are at their healthiest. Both in mind and body.

Do not misunderstand, there is some element of care and concern for our employees. However, try selling an expansion of benefits to your top management (Prince #2) without rationalizing a business justification and you will get tossed out of the board room on your ear. Thus, a healthy, happy, focused, and engaged workforce is much more likely to accomplish corporate goals in a timely and efficient manner than a hurt, broke down, and mentally decrepit workforce. There, that is your bottom-line justification.

Again, HR must buy-in to the mission statement. All HR decisions must align and support the strategic plan as it is written and understood. Being in sync with operations, being an asset to the accomplishment of corporate objectives, and being immersed in the plan, will help HR to be viewed on an equal footing with other departments.

The first step to accomplish this is that HR must come to "understand" the business plan in order to support it. Unfortunately, too many HR practitioners are focused on the administrative duties of the HR function. Not, on the strategic implications of HR alignment. They do not take the time to obtain operational understanding.

For example, delivering a passionate plea for additional human resources funding may be ineffective, unless the HR leader can illustrate to the organization's executive and financial officers the return on investment in HR functions and the resulting impact on the organization's bottom line. An HR practitioner with few leadership skills or who lacks business acumen would likely be unable to make such an argument for additional HR funding.

Further, if HR follows the practices of Prince #1, needs analysis, the potential for going astray and losing the path is greatly reduced.

Additionally, if Prince #1 is applied correctly, then gaining top management buy-in and commitment, Prince #2, is much more likely to be achieved. Thus, if Princes #1 and #2 are properly applied, Prince #3 is probably assured since top management is much more likely to support HR initiatives designed to accomplish corporate goals. These different concepts are intertwined and not mutually exclusive. By following these principles, HR processes are fine tuned to assure that talent is effectively placed, motivated, highly capable and retained.

HR's potential role is huge. HR functions (recruiting and retaining key talent, employee development, performance measurement, motivational culture, etc) span so many different support areas that, if done well, aligning all areas provide a strategic advantage to the organization.

In summary, the test makers love this concept and you may see it repeated in different forms throughout the exam. Just remember the concept of "HR alignment" and you may not only pass your exam but as a bonus, you may become a more valued and respected strategic partner in your organization.

# Practice Quiz (Prince #3):

1.  Which HR activity is of greater strategic value to an organization?
    A.  Emphasizing a progressive recruitment and selection system
    B.  Implementing a comprehensive training program
    C.  Introducing advanced performance appraisal techniques
    D.  Matching HR activities with business strategies

2.  To be viewed as a strategic partner by top management, what is the most crucial action for the HR Manager to take?
    A.  Seek bold and innovative solutions to HR initiatives
    B.  Respond quickly and efficiently to organizational problems
    C.  Offer shared services options
    D.  Ensure HR activities support operational goals

3.  To be most effective in regards to the achievement of operational excellence, HR should strive to:
    A.  Hire the best and brightest
    B.  Align the HR mission with business objectives
    C.  Implement metrics to quantify performance
    D.  Engage and empower workers

4.  The new HR Manager for ABC, Inc. recognizes a disconnect between current HR projects and the functional side of the business. To get back on track, what is the first step the new Manager should take?
    A.  Become familiar with the strategic business plan
    B.  Suspend actions on all current HR projects
    C.  Execute an employee opinion survey for feedback
    D.  Put together a cross-functional team to develop new action plans

5.  Which is the most serious obstacle to HR functioning as an effective ally to business goal accomplishment?
    A.  Operations personnel with closed mindsets
    B.  Poor communications between HR and operations
    C.  HR staff who cannot reason as a business professional
    D.  Under-resourced HR projects

## Answers and explanations:

1   D - Prince #3 demands the correct answer to be, "matching HR activities with business strategies." This is the strategic answer option. Recruiting, training and performance appraisals are considered to be administrative responsibilities of the HR function and more tactical, not as strategic.

2   D - Prince #3 requires the Manager to align HR activities with operational goals. By supporting organizational objectives, HR will make a direct impact on the competitiveness and success of the company and become a strategic partner to top management, and to the other business units.

3   B - Prince #3 defines strategic HR management as the design and implementation of a set of internally consistent practices that ensure an organization's human capital contributes to the business objectives. Aligning the HR mission with the business mission is the most effective approach to business goal achievement.

4   A - First, HR should compare its current strategy with the overall business strategy to determine where the top priorities are not matching up. Prince #3 requires the Manager to align HR activities with the business plan. However, without knowing what the plan is, in detail (Prince #1 - needs analysis), the Manager will not know how to correct course. Therefore, studying the business plan is the first step prior to taking any other action.

5   C - For Prince #3 to work effectively, HR staff must learn to reason and think like business professionals. HR professionals should have a working knowledge of their company and industry. They should understand company finance. They should possess job knowledge of the various organizational positions. They should have a deep understanding of the corporate vision and how HR can help bring about its achievement. Without these business skills, Prince #3 cannot happen... except by luck.

# Prince #4 - Critical Thinking Skills

# (Interpreting, discerning, using judgment)

HR has two primary roles in most organizations. One is strategy focused, as per Prince #3 with HR alignment. The other is administrative. Granted, HR administrates many important functions such as hiring, compensation, record keeping, reviews, training, etc. However, the prevailing perception is that HR is a bunch of clerks processing benefit forms and tracking vacation days. Too focused on compliance and being a cost center to align with the business plan (Prince #3).

To be considered a strategic business partner, HR must escape its reputation as a bunch of mindless, paper pushing Bureaucrats. This blind adherence to policy and procedure is one of the reasons HR reputations sometime suffer. It is easier and safer to bask in the comfortable arms of familiar policies and procedures than making hard and sometimes unpopular decisions that aid the organization's bottom line by being more strategic (Prince #3 again). Regardless, becoming more strategic does not mean that HR can abandon its administrative responsibilities. But to pass the test, you must balance the two.

*Back to business, Prince #4 is focused on having the ability to apply higher order thinking. Higher-order thinking refers to cognitive processes that involve analytical, critical or creative reasoning.*

Without the ability to apply judicious discretion and judgment, passing the HR certification exams is staggeringly difficult. Multiple questions will ask for the "best" answer to a unique, one-off scenario that will require some evaluative thinking.

This creative reasoning should not be ill considered but based on thoughtful and reasoned information. Hopefully, data from a needs analysis (Prince #1) is handy to direct HR activities. If not, the business plan (Prince #3) will form the basis of HR behavior since actions need to be coordinated and aligned with top management goals (Prince #2).

HR candidates must answer different questions using different criteria on the exams. The test taker may only choose from the options given. Sometimes, all of the options appear unlikely in the real world. Or, all could be plausible. That makes no difference. The "best" answer option is the one to choose. Your job is to figure out which it is by weighing the available evidence. Your job is to apply reasonable, reflective thinking based on the best information at hand.

Unfortunately, the ability to evaluate and rationalize the best business solutions are rare skill sets, especially in the field of HR. But to pass these tests, you must develop and hone these abilities. Besides, these skills will aid in your quest to become a strategic partner.

With a complex and rapidly changing workplace, HR professionals are under more pressure than ever to respond and react to a variety of conditions and issues. You must learn to focus on the most relevant information, ask the right questions, separate facts from opinions, make sound decisions and set priorities, regardless of corporate policies and procedures.

So, are you going to be a Bureaucrat or a valued critical thinker? To pass these tests, you will need to develop your decision making, problem solving, and strategic thinking skills. The Seven Princes will help but will not be an answer to all scenario questions.

Clear and reasoned analysis is called for and should be based on the evidence presented and on the key words in the body of the question. And that, my friends, is why you need to study each and every word very carefully. Clues will be provided. A rational answer option will be included but you will have to identify and recognize it.

For example:
What is the best action for the HR Manager to take when a long-term employee, with a solid and squeaky-clean work history, violates an iron-clad attendance policy that requires termination of employment?
    A.   Terminate the employee per company policy
    B.   Find a way to keep the employee and overlook the infraction
    C.   Refer the problem to outside counsel
    D.   Delay action on the matter with the hopes the issue will be
         forgotten

The best answer option is "B." A Bureaucrat would terminate the employee because of strict allegiance to the policy. While a critical thinker would examine the facts and realize this "long-term" employee has been a consistent contributor and needs saving, despite the policy. They would approach the problem with a level of detachment that permits a thorough and balanced analysis. The critical thinker must take the time necessary to make excellent decisions rather than choosing to make fast, good-enough decisions that conform to company guidelines. They seek first to understand (Prince #1) and to find out what they do not know, before making a judgment, so as to make more effective decisions that support the business plan (Prince #3).

I know, I know, some of you are still scratching your head as why policy was bypassed and the employee was not terminated. Let me just say that strict allegiance to the bureaucratic and administrative guidelines may cause a candidate to fail the SPHR exam. You have got to know when and how to evaluate, synthesize and apply discretion if you want to pass these stinking hard tests.

If you did not get the sample question correct, no fears. With practice, you will improve!

As stated earlier, HR's raison d'etre is not purely administrative. A critical thinker is more likely to understand how to apply Prince #3 and reach a state of HR alignment. They know when to follow the rules and when to diverge. They consider all the data and make reasoned choices based on the mitigating factors.

In conclusion, HR leaders must have the ability to apply discretion and judgment (Prince #4) and always put the interests of the company first (Prince #3). Even when it means a standardized approach to talent management may require deviations when extenuating circumstances warrant. Knowing when and where is determined by your critical thinking abilities.

# Practice Quiz (Prince #4):

Use the story to answer the below questions:

**ABC, Inc. has had an unacceptably high turnover rate due to employee dissatisfaction over the harsh policies of a new General Manager. In defense of the Manager, she inherited many issues that include low production levels, subpar quality performance and dissatisfied customers. The prior General Manager was terminated for poor performance and the new GM was brought in to turn around this situation. Additionally, employee engagement is low, absenteeism is high and worker grievance levels are up. Meanwhile, workers compensation claims have risen in recent months and a new competitor for labor has opened in the area and is targeting many of the key employees of ABC.**

1. The HR Manager has just received word that a petition supporting unionization is being passed around in the operations department. Since this is a staunchly union-free facility, the new GM demands to know what the reaction from HR will be. Which action should the HR Manager take?
   A. Call a meeting with employees to address their concerns
   B. Conduct an employee opinion survey
   C. Propose a small across-the-board raise to appease dissatisfaction
   D. Explore possible causes and map response strategies

2. The HR Manager has been contacted privately by a Board Member who asks for the Manager's opinion of the new GM. The best response or position for the HR Manager to take is:
   A. Refuse to get involved
   B. Determine the Board Member's motives and remind them of the chain-of-command process
   C. Answer the Board Member's questions honestly
   D. Speak truthfully only if anonymity is guaranteed

3. The new GM is concerned with her low approval rating. She asks the HR Manager for help. What advice from the HR Manager will be most effective?
   A. Lay low and allow the issues to blow over
   B. Aggressively pursue measures to reduce employee turnover
   C. Openly communicate the necessity of her actions due to organizational challenges
   D. Continue the turnaround process but lighten up on the harsh policies

4. The most effective and strategic action for this HR Manager to take to counter the loss of key employees to the new employer is to:
   A. Share the GM's turnaround vision and convey each employee's role in it
   B. Execute employment contracts on critical employees
   C. Implement a social networking campaign targeting crucial staffers
   D. Offer stay-put bonuses to key personnel

5. Employees are resistant to the changes proposed by the GM. She has become impatient and demands immediate cooperation or threatens drastic actions including mass layoffs. The most appropriate response from the HR Manager is to:
   A. Contact the Board member and report the situation
   B. Urge patience and understanding to give the new plan time to work
   C. Suggest involving employees in creating a path forward
   D. Recommend a leadership development program, with a stress management curriculum, for the GM

## Answers and explanations:

1. D - Since there are varying responses to the situation, Prince #4 requires the HR Manager to apply higher-order thinking to resolve the challenge. In this case, Prince #1 (needs analysis) is an appropriate next step. Options A and B, meeting with employees and conducting an opinion survey (both are forms of needs analysis) may possibly be illegal. The only appropriate next step is to explore the causes and map responses.

2. B - Skip-level questioning, such as this situation, should not be allowed as an opportunity to conduct a witch hunt by the Board Member. It places the HR Manager in an untenable situation. However, if their purpose is honorable, some cooperation may be constructive if it doesn't violate the chain-of-command process. Nevertheless, serious repercussion and tensions could occur from the GM to HR if the Board Member reports and acts on HR's comments and HR fails to inform the GM of the Board Members inquiries.

3. C - Prince #6 explains the importance of open and honest communications in regards to employee relations. This is the best option for the new GM. The other options do not fully address all the production, quality, and customers issues while simultaneously improving employee morale.

4. A - In situations like this, some turnover is inevitable. However, when you give employees the opportunity to understand what they're working for, it creates a sense of purpose and they become more engaged. If workers do not believe in the cause, they will put their hands to work but not their hearts and minds. People become most engaged when they believe in the vision of an organization; when they can make decisions on their own in pursuit of that vision; when they have the skills, knowledge and training necessary to be successful in their roles; and when they understand the purpose of their jobs and how they contribute.

5. C - When resistance is high, performance is low, and profits are sinking, a great response is to promote employee passion and involvement programs (Prince #7). Instead of top-down management, the GM would be wise to overcome resistance with a grass-roots employee involvement program. She will have to delegate authority by spreading out the decision-making process and

encourage input and acceptance from those closest to the problem areas.

# Prince #5 - Most Valuable Assets

## (Every super-villain has to have qualified minions)

Are people really your most important asset? It is almost impossible to find a company that says otherwise, yet few organizations invest as much in their employees as they do in their equipment or processes. Regardless of whether your organization recognizes and reacts to it, your talent is the main strategic advantage your organization has over its competition.

An organization is only as good (or bad) as its workforce. The organization does not generate ideas, provide expertise and ingenuity, or form relations with customers. Workers do it. Thus providing the organization with its most controllable strategic advantage.

The most profound difference between business competitors is in strategy execution. I repeat, strategy execution. Not strategy creation, since all companies have the same ideas and access to the same technologies. Seeing as workers are the key to strategy implementation, they are vital to creating comparative strategic value for the organization. Without creative, committed, engaged, and energetic workers who are focused on accomplishing the organization's mission, you are toast!

The organization's people ultimately determine the effectiveness of strategy development, implementation, and subsequent competitive success. Based on the principle that human capital (employees' collective talents, expertise and qualifications) is an organization's most valuable commodity, strategic human resources leaders need to formulate strategy useful for HR functional and tactical processes. Thus, the test-makers hammer this concept. Expect repeated questions asking what is "most important," and expect the answer to involve an investment in people.

A few examples of the "investments" include: engagement and empowerment initiatives, succession planning, communication (Prince #6 - do not skip ahead, I will get to it later), professional development, and/or participative management styles (Prince #7 - again, later). Though, the exact tool the HR Manager may employ will be determined by a needs analysis (Prince #1) and what they can get approved (Prince #2). Bottom line, the strategic minded organization must be committed to and invest in human capital activities to create and sustain competitive value.

*For those reasons, here is the core learning point for this section; Employees are the organization's "most valuable assets" and should be extended every courtesy and empathy when transgressions arise. Human beings are a strategic advantage for organizations and significant investments of time, training, and money are made in them. Consequently, HR professionals need to work with and support anyone with on-the-job problems or challenges. They are prizes to be protected and developed, not idly thrown away.*

So, if challenged with a situation where an employee is underperforming and action needs to be taken, termination is not usually the correct answer option on these exams. Added training, implement a performance improvement plan (PIP), coach them up, more patience, or possible reassignment to a more suitable position are viable correct answer options on the certification tests. Even the disciplinary process is designed to save misbehaving workers by correcting unacceptable behavior prior to reaching the termination stage.

Also, if employee turnover or dissatisfaction is high, immediate actions and remedies need to be implemented. The organization needs focused and committed workers to carry out the business plan. Thus, the loss of intellectual talent is to be avoided if possible. Besides, replacing workers is extremely expensive. Viable actions include: exit interviews to target causes, review of benefit and reward systems, PIPs, engagement initiatives, and/or employee opinion surveys (Prince #1).

In summary, the "psychological contract" is the unwritten agreement between employee and employer that has as its essence, "You take care of me, and I'll take care of you." In other words, there is a mutual need existing between both parties that they depend on each other to be successful. Thus, workers are treasures to be protected and invested in, rather than to be viewed as a cost item. If they are protected, developed, and aligned with the strategic plan, they may become one of the organization's greatest strategic advantages over its competition and a source of immeasurable strategic value.

Bottom line, and it is true, people really are an organization's most valuable assets! Wow, who knew?!?... the test writers do!

# Practice Quiz (Prince #5):

1. The primary reason to invest in professional development opportunities for organizational talent is to:
   A. Generate earnings
   B. Meet strategic goals
   C. Improve morale
   D. Expand KSA's

2. From a competitive perspective, which is considered the most controllable strategic advantage one organization may have over another?
   A. Human capital
   B. Market share
   C. Corporate flexibility
   D. Product reputation

3. John has been promoted into a new sales leadership position. He is struggling. Departmental performance is down and morale is low. Sales employees are asking for transfers from John's area. John's leadership style is abrasive and confrontational. Management has had enough and realizes an intervention is required. At this point, which action should HR and senior leaders in Sales take?
   A. Terminate and replace John
   B. Put John on a 60-day probation period to turn things around
   C. Require John to take coaching on his performance issues
   D. Document John's shortcomings and begin a confidential search for his replacement

4. Kaplan and Norton's Balanced Scorecard is a strategic planning and management system that is used extensively in business and industry, government, and nonprofit organizations worldwide to align business activities to the vision and strategy of the organization (Prince #3). Which of the four perspectives is oriented to the concept of "knowledge workers?"
   A. Business process
   B. Customer
   C. Financial
   D. Learning & growth

5. The best interpretation of people as a strategic asset is that people are described as being:
   A. Fully engaged and empowered to act independently and with purpose
   B. Creative and innovative in regards to new product and process development
   C. Focused on performing in a manner that implements the firm's strategies
   D. Trained to where their KSA's are aligned with corporate goals

## Answers and explanations:

1  B - The organization's long-term goals (strategic goals) can only be met with human capital (Prince #5) that is ready and capable of executing the firm's plans. While the other answer options are beneficial from a short term (tactical) standpoint, meeting the organization's strategic goals (Prince #3) by aligning the most critical elements to goal accomplishment (human capital - Prince #5) is crucial.

2  A - Prince #5 finds that human capital (the set of marketable skills employees posses that allows them to be productive) is a more controllable competitive advantage than the other answer options. Further, Prince #5 says that employees are the most important source of wealth for any organization. Without creative and innovative thought leaders, the organization will be stuck at its present stage of development and will be unable to respond and react to strategic business opportunities that may occur.

3  C - Prince #5 postulates that since John is new in the position, he must be developed and coached. His coaching should not be punitive but growth oriented. He must be given time to settle into the position while supported with resources and the opportunity to grow into the role. There was a reason John was promoted. He must have some skills and the potential to become a leadership asset of the organization.

4  D - The Learning and Growth perspective (which is aligned Prince #5 theory) includes employee training and corporate cultural attitudes related to both individual and corporate self-improvement. In a knowledge-worker organization (Prince #5), people -- the only repository of knowledge -- are the main resource. Learning and growth constitute the essential foundation for success of any knowledge-worker organization.

5  C - Remembering that Prince #5 identifies people as the most important assets as they are the ones who must act and behave strategically by carrying out the duties of, and aligning with, the firm's strategies (Prince #3) allows you to find the best answer.

# Prince #6 - Communication

## (The heir to the throne)

A great communications program is the heart and soul of HR relations. It drives business results.

Without good communications, HR has zero chance of informing, involving and aligning workers in the accomplishment of organizational goals (Prince #3). Therefore, the glue that holds together the mission, the vision, and the team is communications... every single time.

There is an old saying in golf that good putting cures all ills. In HR, good communication cures all ills. Almost every challenge faced by HR leaders can be resolved with effective exchanges of information with workers. So, your lesson for this section, my scholarly pupil, if you see communications as an answer option, choose it... above all others.

A more descriptive title for the HR Manager may be "Communications Manager." If, per Prince #5, people are the most important assets, keeping them engaged and empowered starts with keeping them informed and listening to what they have to say. This is never more true than during change initiatives.

Thus, HR departments that do a good job of blending change strategy with communications strategy will be far more successful. Advantages include: better employee/employer relations, lessens confrontations and misunderstandings, better productivity, clearer goal setting, helps shape realistic expectations, etc.

Without a defined and effective communications strategy, especially during periods of transition (layoffs, mergers/acquisitions, leadership changes, changes to the mission, etc.), the organization will struggle. Communications is the conduit by which change happens. With it, HR can lower turnover, improve efficiency, and align HR (Prince #3). Without it, forget it!

Examples of HR communication techniques include: online conversations, briefs, meetings, suggestion systems, fireside chats, informal conversations, newsletters, emails, texts, virtual town hall meetings, open door policies, etc.. Some of these techniques are downward and some are upward. But the best forms of communication are two-way. For example, a brief usually morphs into a Q&A when clear and open communication is being utilized.

The communications strategy and its techniques for execution are often a reflection of the corporate culture. Traditionally, management controlled all aspects of communications. Both formal and informal. Now, employees communicate informally 24/7 with modern technology. HR has had to adapt and keep up or get lost in the dust, constantly playing catch-up.

Progressive HR departments are using social media to recruit, inform, recognize accomplishments and engage workers. These communication systems have the power to reach most workers simultaneously, across borders and time zones. However, not everyone is receptive to these changes.

Multi-cultural workforces are especially challenging. Different nationalities think differently, solve problems differently, and communicate differently. Even different generations communicate differently. The challenge for the HR leader is to overcome these issues and reconcile the group into a high performing work team.

Honesty and transparency are keys to building a good foundation for communications. Especially with a multi-cultural workforce. Direct and honest feedback is an essential tool for the HR leader. Communications is not always polite conversation. It is often about the difficult message, such as employee feedback, discipline, performance improvements... While no one likes playing the bad-guy, clear communications are essential for behavior correction. The progressive leader must clearly and factually give examples of unacceptable behaviors and the necessary steps to performance improvement. Further, good communications strategy demands the actions be formalized through documentation.

Again, there will be difficult conversations for the HR professional and they must embrace this role. Usually, an honest and straightforward approach that is free from personal bias is best. No one likes confrontation. However, sweeping confrontation under the rug is anathema to Prince #3 (alignment). It is necessary and vital to the health of the organization. This way, respect will be earned and trust gained.

In summary, new programs and initiatives do not usually fail due to poor design. They usually fail due to poor execution. Poor execution is often attributed to poor communications. Thus, proper communications have a positive effect on execution and morale. Since communication systems form the fabric of success, they are not just a Prince but may be the future King.

# Practice Quiz (Prince #6):

1. The most important HR responsibility during a corporate change initiative is:
   A. Implementation
   B. Policy alignment
   C. Personnel assignments
   D. Communication

2. ABC, Inc. has a goal of retaining 100% of the employees of an organization they are acquiring. To assist in this goal, which is most effective during the integration phase for the HR team?
   A. Communication
   B. Stock options
   C. Due diligence
   D. Retention bonuses

3. The HR Manager anticipates a great amount of resistance to a new reward system top management has designed to replace the current and popular program. To enhance acceptance, what must the HR Manager's most important focus be before, during and after the plan rollout?
   A. Employee empowerment
   B. Communicating the message, purpose and methods
   C. Benchmark data sets to local industry norms
   D. Speed of implementation

4. Two departments return performance appraisals that vary significantly in terms of rating consistency. What is the BEST action the HR department can take to level set performance ratings?
   A. Provide training and communication on expectations
   B. Use process metrics to identify inconsistencies
   C. Use consistent language in comments
   D. Implement a checklist/matrix rating system

5. Jasmine has been the HR Manager at the 200 person ABC, Inc. for six months. She has been directed by top management to cut the workforce by 8% while minimizing dissatisfaction by the non-affected. Which communications approach will be most effective at accomplishing her goals?
   A. Private correspondence to the affected during non-working hours
   B. Social media announcement that allows online feedback
   C. General announcement by CEO followed by 1-on-1 meetings with supervisory staff
   D. HR representatives to meet with all 200 employees 1-on-1

## Answers and explanations:

1. D - Prince #6 advises the HR department to focus on establishing an effective communications program during periods of organizational change. Employees need information to aid engagement, reduce fear of the unknown and to foster acceptance. Without the free flow of information to employees, they may distrust intentions, hinder implementation and disrupt performance.

2. A - Knowledge is power (Prince #6)! Because a strong communication program is critical during the early integration phase to achieve retention goals, the HR staff must focus on presenting detailed information and updates to allay the fears and concerns of the acquired company staffers. HR must act to reduce the disruption and anxiety of the transition process for the new employees by meeting with and communicating the important topics of salary, benefits, work assignment, job continuity, etc.

3. B - While all answer options have some merit, communicating the message is the critical component (Prince #6) in overcoming resistance and gaining acceptance. Without explaining the purpose and methods to employees, they will not readily trust its intent. It is better to provide them with the unvarnished truth, even when painful, than allowing them to make uninformed assumptions.

4. A - is correct per Prince #6 (communications). Unless managers and employees have a solid and shared understanding of performance rating scales and the performance expectations, the organization will never achieve fairness and consistency in employee performance appraisals. The other answer options provide some benefit to bringing consistency but "training and communicating expectations" is the best answer.

5. C - Top management commitment is demonstrated by the CEO's general announcement (Prince #2). Plus, employees need to hear from their supervisor how the change will affect them and why this layoff is necessary to accomplish the goals of the organization (Prince #3). Employees want to hear these important facts from their direct chain-of-command (Prince #6), not the HR department.

# Prince #7 - Employee Participation

## (You want it solved, get them involved)

If employees are truly the most important commodity (Prince #5) in the accomplishment of organizational goals, motivating their alignment (Prince #3) is a paramount need (Prince #1). HR professionals have long recognized the benefits of involvement programs. They have a huge impact on goal accomplishment. Participation programs include allowing worker involvement in corporate governance, decision making, problem solving, direction setting, and customer interaction. By doing so, the organization has a greater probability of attaining employee: acceptance, support, engagement and empowerment... not to mention better morale.

Corporations are constantly faced with difficult challenges, change initiatives, market pressures, or just plain employee resistance. An organized and formal employee involvement program is often the solution. In essence, employees want a say in setting the direction of the organization. Especially in those areas that affect their work life. And, when they get it, they are much more likely to support a strategic initiative they helped plan and implement.

Simply put, no taxation without representation. Everybody needs to sing off the same page of the hymn book. Harness the power of the masses instead of the few. Many hands make light work. Two heads are better than one... Got it now? Good!

The path to ingenuity, efficiency, productivity, motivation, and commitment starts and ends with employee involvement. Common techniques employed are: TQM, Lean Manufacturing, Six Sigma, round tables, ESOPs, feedback/suggestion systems, reward systems tied to corporate goals, etc. Also, weave the company's values and goals into employees' performance appraisals. This will enhance the probability that employee-led initiatives are both productive and align with the strategic plans. Make an effort to recognize or reward employees who are particularly successful. Thanking employees for their burst of creativity or hard work will help reinforce the shared values.

*All of these activities have employee engagement at its heart. Thus, the core reason for an organization to adopt an employee participation initiative is to seek a committed, supportive and loyal workforce.*

To clarify, "engagement" is the goal of involvement programs. Not necessarily "empowerment." These two terms are often confused and interchanged but that is a mistake. Workers can be engaged (committed and loyal) but not empowered (autonomous and self-directed). Or, they can be empowered without being engaged. It is most desirable when they are both engaged and empowered but that unfortunately is not always the case.

Your take-away from this section, young disciple, is the way to solve most acceptance problems, or a lack of motivation, or stilted thought leadership, is to turn to your employees. Give them a chance. The benefits are many-fold. The detriments of not involving them is often devastating. So, any question that asks how to improve efficiency, effectiveness, productivity, motivation, acceptance, engagement, empowerment, or quality, usually involves employee involvement (pun intended).

# Practice Quiz (Prince #7):

1.  When considering a new professional development program targeting first-level leaders, the Training Manager recognizes which action will be most effective for gaining trust and cooperation from this group?
    A.  Personally ask a few respected executives to support the new program
    B.  Integrate some first level leaders into the design team
    C.  Add the new training curriculum to the rated categories on their appraisals
    D.  Provide a financial incentive for completing the training curriculum

2.  In regards to employee engagement, common business theory assumes when workers take on real decision-making authority:
    A.  Demand for greater autonomy is reduced
    B.  Their commitment to the organization and its goals increase
    C.  Effective decision-making drops, while engagement increases
    D.  Engagement decreases, while empowerment increases

3.  A new and costly material handling process has been implemented in the Shipping department. Despite the proven efficiencies of this new system, it is apparent most workers are continuing to use the old techniques. Change-management theory predicts this outcome due to:
    A.  Organized labor opposition due to feather-bedding concerns
    B.  Improper work-load balancing
    C.  Employees were not allowed input into the changes
    D.  Sufficient leadership support was lacking

4.  Which is not a common tool for enhancing employee involvement and participation?
    A.  Lean Manufacturing
    B.  ESOP
    C.  TQM
    D.  Production incentives

5. Which is the MOST critical element of an individual development plan?
   A. Two way commitment between employee and manager
   B. Identifying development actions
   C. Assessing current strengths
   D. Put the plan in writing

## Answers and explanations:

1. B - Involving the leaders in the design and development of the program will enhance their acceptance and trust per Prince #7. Resistance and opposition should be reduced and acceptance enhanced with their participation. Further, the program should be based on a needs analysis (Prince #1). Thus, more alignment with the business plan (Prince #3). And, easier to get funded (Prince #2).

2. B - Engagement theory predicts enhanced commitment and loyalty with increased employee authority (Prince #7). As workers become more empowered, in regards to decision making, they will take on more ownership and become greater stake-holders in the organization's success or failure.

3. C - Prince #7 would predict this outcome due to the failure to involve the Shippers who are expected to carry out the changes. While their participation is not a 100% guarantee of success, it will improve the likelihood of a favorable outcome by leaps and bounds.

4. D - Lean, ESOP (Employee Stock Ownership Plans), and TQM (Total Quality Management) are all systems that rely on employees contributing to the cause. These programs facilitate the concept of the employee as a stakeholder in the process (Prince #7). Production incentives, not as directly. Production incentives require a financial reward for increased output. This may be achieved individually and without any change in employee participation.

5. A - Developing the IDP is a collaborative effort between the employee and the manager. Without a commitment from both, the plan has little chance to succeed. For the employee to develop, both the supervisor and the employee must be involved in assessing current skills, path forward scheduling of developmental opportunities, identifying and approving the expenditure of money and resources, analyzing current and future organizational needs and opportunities, etc. While the employee is the owner of the plan and the person most responsible, it is a two-way collaboration between employee and supervisor. Therefore, this is an example of Prince #7 - getting workers involved.

# Case Study

OK, let's test what you can remember and apply regarding the 7 Princes. I'm going to give you a case study and then ask you some questions. It is a great way to practice and improve Prince #4, critical thinking skills. You'll need these kind of experiences to survive the case studies on the actual exams. Remember, everything in HR is not always clear cut and some situations require you to use the 7 Princes. OK, let's go.

**ABC, Inc. is a manufacturer of roller bearings. It has been in business for 25 years and most of the workforce is unionized. It has several locations around the world but the headquarters is located in the United States. Its products are made to exacting tolerances and must be closely monitored to ensure they meet standards.**

**Rashmi has been employed for three years as a Quality Engineer at ABC, Inc. He was transferred from the New Delhi location to HQ three years ago. His office is located next to the production area for easy access when his support is needed. While he is not needed in the manufacturing area continuously, when he is needed, it is usually an immediate requirement to limit production interruptions.**

**However, he suffers from severe migraines which he claims are aggravated and triggered by noise from the plant floor. He has seen a Physician who has provided written direction that Rashmi be provided a noise-free work area.**

**Rashmi has requested a new office on the opposite side of the facility, away from the manufacturing area and the noise. Rashmi's management team believes Rashmi may be using the entire situation for his own personal reasons and they do not want to comply with his requests.**

Before you start answering questions, let us examine the situation. From information given, can you assume Rashmi is an underperformer?... No, the write up does not indicate he is a problem employee. Therefore, my advice, apply Prince #5 (most valuable asset) throughout the questions. And, it may be a different story if he had been described as an under-achiever with several disciplinary actions against him and poor performance reviews. If that's not indicated, then we want to treat him like he is the golden child.

# Practice Quiz (Case Study):

1. When considering whether to work with or against Rashmi's wishes, what must be the first consideration for the HR Manager?
   A. Management's opinion
   B. Rashmi's opinion
   C. Legal compliance
   D. Organizational policy

2. From the information provided, is Rashmi entitled to protection and reasonable accommodation from the Americans with Disabilities Act (ADA)?
   A. No, he is not a U.S. citizen
   B. No, migraines are not protected under ADA
   C. No, since an office relocation is considered unreasonable for migraines
   D. Probably

3. If a legal determination is made that Rashmi's migraines must be treated as an ADA issue, what is the next step the HR Manager should take?
   A. Communicate with the leadership team on the company's obligations
   B. Transfer Rashmi's office
   C. Offer Rashmi ear plugs versus the office relocation
   D. Redesign Rashmi's job to avoid the production area

4. If the office transfer is turned down, Rashmi has requested to be allowed to work from home as he believes that to be a reasonable accommodation for his migraines. What should the employer do?
   A. Deny the request
   B. Collaborate with Rashmi to find common ground
   C. Grant the original request for an office transfer
   D. Refer the matter to legal counsel

5. Rashmi claims that his many absences, leave-earlies and frequent tardiness should be recorded as intermittent FMLA leave even though his supervisor believes it to be a convenient excuse. What should the HR Manager do?
   A. Comply with company policy and FMLA regulations, despite the suspicions
   B. Require him to see the company Doctor when his absences are suspect
   C. Patiently wait for him to exhaust his FMLA leave allotment and then terminate him
   D. Require him to provide qualified medical direction that supports his claim

6. In this case, if Rashmi were to apply for Workers Compensation, should the HR Manager approve it?
   A. Yes, due to the noise aggravating his migraines
   B. No, due to the migraines being unrelated to the job
   C. Yes, because his migraines are caused by the plant noise
   D. No, because his migraines are a preexisting condition

7. While off work one day for intermittent leave, Rashmi posts a picture on social media of him skiing at a local resort. Now, what should the employer do?
   A. Terminate Rashmi for fraud
   B. Call Rashmi into HR and discipline him for abusing his FMLA leave
   C. Meet with Rashmi and discuss the situation and possible resolution
   D. Ignore the picture as the employer may not dictate an employee's action while on leave

# Answers and explanations:

1. C - Prince #1 believes that every process should begin with a needs analysis. Complying with the local laws is the largest "need" the HR Manager and the organization has. While the other answer options must be dealt with at some point in the process, the legal requirements trump the others and must come first.

2. D - This case is not clear cut... that is why you are getting it. It may or may not be an ADA protected issue. Thus, Prince #4 must be applied. Under ADA and the stricter ADAAA guidelines, employers should be cautious and err on the side of considering most impairments to be disabilities and attempting accommodation. It is more difficult than ever before for an employer to successfully assert that a physical or mental impairment is not a disability, and employers must instead focus on whether they are required to make reasonable accommodations for disabled employees in order that they may perform their essential job functions.

3. A - Prince #2 requires the HR Manager to seek management's buy-in and support before taking any further actions. Additionally, Prince #7 applies to leaders as well and they need to be involved in finding a solution since they suspect Rashmi of shirking.

4. B - Employers are not required to provide each and every accommodation that is requested, only a reasonable one. However, Prince #7 would want Rashmi to be actively involved in finding an acceptable resolution that all parties could live with. Further, Prince #6 believes that by communicating openly and honestly with Rashmi, his resistance will be lessened and a mutual agreement is more likely.

5. D - Since Rashmi is a valued asset (Prince #5), he should be treated with trust and respect until proven otherwise. However, the HR Manager should not turn a blind eye to the supervisor's suspicions. Thus, determining the medical necessity (Prince #1) must occur first before any other action may be taken. After a Doctor's note is obtained, further responses must be based on competent medical opinion... not on the supervisor's judgment because I doubt he went to medical school... but anything is possible.

6. A - Workers Compensation law requires coverage for medical conditions that are aggravated by on-the-job conditions. In this case,

Rashmi is most probably entitled to Work Comp coverage if the employer does not heed the Doctor's orders to remove him from the noisy work area.

7. C - Unfortunately, if you are looking for a clear cut answer, you will not find one. The employer is not allowed to retaliate against Rashmi for exercising his FMLA rights. However, skiing is not consistent with someone who is having an incapacitating migraine. Since Rashmi is a treasured asset (Prince #5), the best solution is to work it out with him (Prince #6 and #7) and comply with medical opinion and company guidelines.

# Practice Quiz

## (All Princes)

*By practicing the application of the Seven Princes, they will become second nature and many of the elusive questions on the certification exams will be simplified. Good luck!*

1.  Human assets rise to the level of a strategic asset when they:
    A.  Are trained and developed to meet corporate standards
    B.  Align with tactical and operational needs
    C.  Are committed and flexible in achieving corporate goals
    D.  Become a source of competitive advantage

2.  The most probable guarantor of success and acceptance, for a newly proposed compensation plan, is:
    A.  Support from quantifiable market-area survey data
    B.  Employee involvement at the development stage
    C.  Highly committed management members to the project
    D.  Full communications at every stage of program design

3.  Employees are nervous and concerned due to rumors of the possible loss of a major contract that may have staffing consequences. To alleviate the stress of the situation, which action should HR recommend?
    A.  No action necessary at this point
    B.  Communicate the known facts to the employees
    C.  Deny the rumors
    D.  Conduct a series of 1-on-1 meetings with all employees

4.  In regards to the employee, the strategic HR leader will MOST probably seek:
    A.  Better control
    B.  Conformity
    C.  Speed and effectiveness
    D.  Commitment

5. After several false starts, the Safety Manager at ABC, Inc. has been asked to initiate a new accident reduction program that is targeted and specific to the lowest performing departments. Which action should the Manager begin with?
   A. Seek approval to implement a safety incentive program
   B. Conduct a gap analysis on all departments
   C. Create a cross-functional implementation team to enhance employee acceptance
   D. Obtain budgetary guidelines and approvals

6. The HR Manager at ABC, Inc. needs to develop and submit the HR department's annual plan of work to top management for review and approval. To enhance its acceptance, how should the plan be primarily originated?
   A. By conducting an environmental scan
   B. Through comparison to industry best practices
   C. From a consultative process with HR staff members
   D. With a review of the organization's strategic business plan

7. With limited resources, finances and time, the HR Manager at ABC, Inc. must prioritize her departmental projects. What action should she take first?
   A. Seek top management commitment
   B. Establish the communications plan
   C. Obtain further financial funding
   D. Determine organizational needs

8. With limited resources, finances and time, the HR Manager at ABC, Inc. must prioritize her departmental projects. During this process, what is her most important task?
   A. Conducting an analysis of project criteria
   B. Obtaining additional funding
   C. Seeking and obtaining executive support
   D. Creating an action plan

9. Winston is a promising young Engineer. Lately, there have been rumors of his having alcohol breath when he returns from lunch. When confronted, he admits to drinking at lunch but denies he has a substance abuse problem. What should be the next step for the HR Manager?
   A. Require Winston to meet with EAP consultants for evaluation
   B. Since he hasn't tested positive and impairment wasn't reported, no action
   C. Require Winston to submit to weekly drug and alcohol testing
   D. Follow company policy and terminate Winston

10. From the HR viewpoint, the most critical element of a successful new project introduction is:
    A. Employee training
    B. Reward system alignment
    C. Talent
    D. Communication

11. Off to a shaky start with a new performance management system due to widespread resistance, it is most essential and effective for the HR Manager to seek:
    A. A quantifiable analysis of progress to date
    B. More active involvement from organizational management
    C. One-on-one meetings with key opposition leaders
    D. A program redesign to address concerns

12. With poor morale crippling operational performance at ABC, Inc., the HR Manager has been tasked with addressing and reversing the current state. What is not an opening step the Manager should take?
    A. Conduct an organizational assessment
    B. Execute an employee opinion survey
    C. Grant an across-the-board pay raise
    D. Review recent exit interview feedback

13. Despite best efforts, employee morale at ABC, Inc. continues to suffer due to recent cutbacks and a reorganization. Which is not an effective action the HR leader can take to counter this?
    A. Grant an across-the-board increase to all
    B. Put together a cross functional employee relations team to propose solutions
    C. Conduct an opinion survey to focus a response plan
    D. Identify and implement an engagement initiative

14. The current benefits package at ABC, Inc. is considered out of date and a liability in attracting and retaining top talent. What action should the Benefits Manager should take in advance of redesigning ABC's offerings?
    A. List the services for bid with local agents
    B. Seek support from the executive team
    C. Communicate the proposed changes to the workforce
    D. Dissect the shortcomings of the current program

15. The most essential skill for a great HR leader is:
    A. Delegation
    B. Being organized
    C. Communication
    D. Administrative

16. Resistance to a new sales commission plan is high among the sales staff. In hindsight, the Compensation Manager realizes the most effective approach to gaining staff acceptance would have been to:
    A. Place a few sales department employees on the design team
    B. Use industry accepted benchmark data
    C. Gain top managers prior commitment
    D. Align the new plan with the business goals

17. Which is the first question a Sales Representative from ABC, Inc. should ask a prospective new customer?
    A. What were your purchasing levels last quarter?
    B. How much are you currently paying for these items?
    C. What are the business goals you require to be supported?
    D. Who are your current vendors?

18. The most effective way to get a stalled HR project back on track due to departmental infighting is to:
    A. Assign more resources
    B. Relax budgetary restrictions
    C. Communicate the benefits of the program
    D. Get supportive executives to play a more active role

19. For the HR practitioner, establishing and maintaining a superior communications program is most challenging in which type organization?
    A. Hierarchical structure
    B. Start-up
    C. Multi-cultural workforce
    D. Matrix

20. What is the first step in the strategic planning process?
    A. Assigning responsibilities
    B. Setting the objectives
    C. Evaluating different approaches
    D. Balancing input

21. What is the primary purpose for aligning business and HR strategies?
    A. To gain broader acceptance from operational staff
    B. To secure and sustain a competitive commercial advantage
    C. It aids in obtaining top management commitment
    D. To secure a seat at the strategy planning table for HR

22. The HR Manager at ABC, Inc. has been directed to design and implement a new performance measurement system for the customer service representatives. Management wishes to empower the Reps to respond quickly to customer concerns and then measure their success. In addition to the measurement system, which must accompany this program for its most effective launch?
    A. Qualitative baseline data
    B. An increase in rewards/compensation
    C. KSA training
    D. Both financial and non-financial analysis

23. Jesper has been underperforming and his manager needs to execute a PIP with him before more serious issues occur. He does not usually receive constructive criticism well. The most effective approach for the Manager to take with Jesper is to:
    A. Avoid this confrontation and wait for more actionable violations
    B. Threaten him with more serious discipline if behaviors are not corrected
    C. Ask him to conduct a self-review
    D. Give Jesper specific examples of his underperformance

24. Which action(s) should HR take to earn the highest measures of organizational respect?
    A. Measure its effectiveness in terms of business competitiveness
    B. Enhance employee satisfaction by encouraging more employee autonomy
    C. Implement programs to enhance employee engagement
    D. Install operational systems that facilitate employee good will

25. In an hierarchical organization, which is the most essential element to obtain prior to introducing a new HR initiative?
    A. Senior level buy-in
    B. Bottom-up feedback and participative involvement
    C. Qualifiable data to support plan goals
    D. Contingency plans as to not waste company resources

26. An organization that recognizes its intellectual assets to be of strategic value would most probably initiate which of the following concepts?
    A. Product differentiation
    B. Learning culture
    C. Employment branding initiatives
    D. Promotion-from-within policies

27. Which is most effective at forming the foundation for successful teamwork and aligns the organizational purpose to the human participants?
    A. Training
    B. Planning
    C. Assigning
    D. Communicating

28. Much research exists that identifies which element as the key differentiator as to whether a firm's strategic plan accomplishes its goals?
   A. People
   B. Market place competition
   C. Professional development
   D. Organizational flexibility

29. Despite the lack of a management champion, and with no functional budget, the HR Manager at ABC, Inc. is determined to move forward with her new professional development plan. She intends to redirect funds from other HR program as she considers the development initiative vital to achieving departmental and organizational goals. The next step the HR Manager should take is:
   A. Abandon all actions while lobbying for management support
   B. Form a cross-functional team to develop an implementation plan
   C. Enlist volunteers to beta-test the proposed program
   D. Notify HR staffers of changes to HR budgetary restrictions

30. Under management pressure to increase output, and out of innovative ideas, the departmental supervisor would produce the most effective results by:
   A. Implementing a cost-cutting initiative
   B. Hire consultants with efficiency expertise
   C. Benchmark competitors
   D. Involve workers in producing solutions

31. While executing a departmental review that is critical of performance and results, the most effective method to ensure the message is delivered is to:
   A. Present factual examples
   B. Tie future rewards to on-the-job behavior
   C. Promise disciplinary action for departmental employees if improvements are not immediate
   D. Discuss the issues in a non-confrontational and general manner

32. For the HR function to have the greatest impact on an organization's value creation, it must:
   A. Quantify HR services in regards to industry best practices
   B. Focus efforts on staffing the best and brightest
   C. Ensure human assets are coordinated with the business strategy
   D. Implement cutting edge performance management systems

33. The Learning & Growth Perspective of Kaplan and Norton's Balanced Scorecard focuses on the internal skills and capabilities of the employees that are required to support value-creating internal processes. Which is not a common metric used to evaluate the Learning and Growth perspective?
    A. Training dollars per employee
    B. Employee productivity
    C. Employee turnover
    D. Operations cost

Use the following story to answer the next three questions:

**The HR Manager at ABC, Inc. receives a letter from an ex-employee's Attorney stating they are suing ABC for sexual harassment. The allegation is the employee's immediate supervisor was a bit too touchy-feely. The Manager is caught by surprise. She has had no prior knowledge of this issue and is confused since the ex-employee voluntarily resigned, with notice, two months earlier. Additionally, the supervisor is a long-term leader with an excellent reputation. The employee had been a model worker and while the resignation came as a surprise, she never mentioned harassment during the exit interview. The Attorney is demanding a settlement of $500,000 plus attorney fees to end this matter.**

34. What is the best initial response the HR Manager can give to the plaintiffs attorney?
    A. No response is mandated, let them make the next move
    B. Inform the Attorney the ex-employee had voluntarily quit and the claim is meritless
    C. Refer the Attorney to in-house counsel
    D. The company takes the complaint seriously and will respond after an investigation

35. After receiving the complaint, what should the HR Manager do first?
    A. Begin an investigation into the allegations
    B. Turn the matter over to in-house counsel
    C. Suspend the supervisor until the matter is settled
    D. Respond to the Attorney's letter seeking clarification

36. The Attorney requests a copy of the employee's personnel file, what action should the HR Manager take?
    A. Send a copy of all items in the file
    B. Deny the request without a court order
    C. Follow company policy and respond accordingly
    D. Require the ex-employee to personally make the request

# Answers:

1.  D - Intellectual assets are strategic assets when they become a source of competitive advantage (Prince #5). While the other answer options are desirable, they are stages on the path to becoming a strategic asset. Once the employees offer the employer a competitive advantage, then they offer strategic value.

2.  C - Prince #2 believes that highly committed management will be the key to acceptance and success for a new compensation plan. If top management believes the program to be important, resources will be allocated and obstacles removed. While top management commitment does not guarantee employee acceptance, it does provide a suitable foundation upon which to build favorable employee tolerance.

3.  B - Prince #6 postulates that honesty is the best policy for a situation like this. Transparency and openness will replace the fear of the unknown with factual information. Even negative information is preferable to no information. Princes #5 and #6 believe people are assets who will handle the possibility of change better if provided with clear and candid insight.

4.  D - "Commitment" is the correct answer. Forward thinking leaders will attempt to empower employees to seek ownership of the task or process. This creates a deep dedication to solving and improving the process. Control, conformity, and speed are qualities associated with tactical management of the worker. Prince #7, employee participation, is a common way to develop committed employees.

5.  B - A gap analysis is used to compare actual business performance with ideal performance and is a form of a "needs analysis" - Prince #1. Gap analysis is considered a benchmarking tool for efficiency and is used for outlining a clearer road map for future growth, and can be used at both the strategic and operational levels of an organization. In short, it tries to fill the "gap" between where a company is, and where it aims to be.

6.  D - Prince #3 postulates HR departments will derive their goals from the business objectives of the organization to become more strategically involved. In order for the HR plan of work to be most accepted by top management, it should correspond and support the strategic needs of the organization and its business plan.

7.  D - Prince #1 requires a "needs analysis" as the first step in determining and ordering departmental priorities... always!

8.  C - Prince #2 will always identify the solicitation of top management commitment as the most important task during the planning stages. Without executive buy-in, the Manager must not waste her precious few resources on non-supported projects.

9.  A - Since Prince #5 identifies Winston as a valued asset, and no contrary information was provided, the next logical step is to refer him to the EAP specialists for evaluation and possible intervention. There was not enough information provided in the question to require any of the other answer options to be acted upon.

10. D - Prince #6 will predict the new introduction will have great difficulty without an effective communication program to support it. Whether employees needing information, customers, or vendors, good communications is the key to a successful launch.

11. B - Prince #2 holds that obtaining more active involvement from top leaders would send a strong and clear message that this new system is supported at the highest levels. Additionally, their support will be most essential and effective in reducing any organized resistance. Should top managers vigorously serve as supportive role models, the probability of acceptance is greatly enhanced.

12. C - Per the steps in the ADDIE model, the first step in any process is to study the causal reasons for the problem and then to shape a reaction. Per Prince #1, the "needs assessment" is required in this case to identify performance requirements and the knowledge, skills, and abilities needed by an agency's workforce to achieve the requirements. Since morale is an "ability," an effective training needs assessment will help direct resources to areas of greatest demand. All of the answer options are examples of needs assessments except, "granting a pay raise," since it may not be identified as a causal factor.

13. A - Prince #7 predicts involving the workers in the solution will produce the best results. Your critical thinking analysis (Prince #4) should have told you the raise was the incorrect answer option. The company is cutting back (layoff) and probably will not have any extra money for raises. Asking top management for a raise during

an economic downturn is a violation of Prince #2 (commitment) and is a fool's mission.

14. D - Prince #1 requires that a needs analysis be conducted prior to initiating any actions towards updating the benefits program. An analysis of what ABC currently has versus what they need must occur prior to the beginning of the redesign process. In this example, dissecting and identifying the current shortcomings is a necessary first step.

15. C - Great HR professionals must have great communications skills (Prince #6 - remember the heir apparent). The modern HR leader is at the center of the organizational communications management process.

16. A - Prince #7 would predict resistance in this situation. A more effective approach would have been to involve the sales staff in the design and implementation. While the other answer options have merit, resistance is overcome with participation and involvement.

17. C - The first step in any process is to conduct a needs analysis - Prince #1. The best question(s) to ask a new prospect is/are questions that identify the needs of the customer's organization. Then, the next step is to link a method as to how ABC, Inc. can support these operational goals - Prince #3, but that was not the question. Remember to answer the question asked. Not the one you "think" they asked.

18. D - Prince #2 holds that obtaining more active involvement from top leaders would send a strong and clear message that this new system is supported at the highest levels. Additionally, their support will be most essential and effective in reducing any organized resistance. Should top managers vigorously serve as supportive role models, the probability of acceptance is greatly enhanced.

19. C - Communications systems (Prince #6) are especially important and challenging in multi-cultural workplaces (national origin, generational, religious, etc.). Different cultures communicate differently. While there are many benefits to a multi-cultural workforce, getting all parties to listen and understand each other is a major task.

20. B - The first step in any process is to conduct a needs analysis - Prince #1. The needs analysis will determine the plan's objectives. If it is not needed, it should not be in the plan. Prior to any other activity, the objectives must be set or resources will be wasted.

21. B - Per Prince #3, when HR is properly aligned, it contributes to a successful business strategy and the financial bottom line. It helps secure and sustain a competitive advantage. While the other answer options have value, the primary reason for aligning HR is for business and financial achievement.

22. C - Without the skills to be an independent and empowered decision-maker, it will be fruitless to measure their performance. Only mature, trained and experienced workers should be expected to operate independently and autonomously (Prince #7). Skills training usually goes hand-in-hand with an expansion of power and self-direction.

23. D - Prince #6 provides that specific and factual examples of his performance is a superior form of communication when a confrontation is expected. This approach will be most effective at lessening his resistance by demonstrating there is no personal animus and the PIP is in his best interests.

24. A - Prince #3 forces HR to understand that to contribute in a strategic manner, it must earn respect. To earn respect, it must measure its effectiveness in terms of business competitiveness, rather than employee feelings. HR must coordinate all its activities to support the business plan and improve organizational capacity. Again, if HR wants to respected as a business partner, then it must measure itself in a business manner.

25. A - Top-down reporting relationships are typical in an hierarchical organization. Therefore, it is essential to obtain top management commitment prior to launching any new endeavor. Prince #2 proposes that without senior level support prior to project initiation, failure is likely.

26. B - Organizations that recognize the value of Prince #5 as a strategic advantage, will invest in their workers to develop their KSA's. Firms with learning cultures continuously develop the skills needed to succeed in their market. Learning cultures help employees find a sense of purpose in the organization and it helps them rise to their

level of potential in assisting the organization to achieve its long-term goals... thus, the strategic value.

27. D - Prince #6 (communications) is by far the most important element to great teamwork. Without good communications, the individuals cannot form themselves into a successful and cohesive unit. Further, without a solid communication system, accomplishing and aligning talent with organizational goals (Prince #3) is unlikely.

28. A - Employees are a strategic asset (Prince #5) because people play the critical role in plan creation and implementation. The ability to execute strategy properly is one of the primary differentiators between companies. Further, it is a source of competitive value. People are crucial to business plan execution. The inability to execute the line of attack well is one of the most common reasons for strategic plan failure... and it is one of the most common reasons why CEO's get fired.

29. A - Without a champion from the executive team (Prince #2), this proposal has little chance to succeed. Despite the worthwhile intentions of the HR Manager, she should shelve the idea until, and if, she can garner support from a senior leader.

30. D - Since the supervisor is out of ideas, she should turn to the workers and involve them in creating the solution (Prince #7). They are most familiar with the process and have the greatest level of expertise. By involving them, she may generate fresh ideas, decrease resistance to change, and obtain the results management seeks.

31. A - Prince #6 predicts that clear and direct communications are essential for behavior correction. The progressive leader must clearly and factually give examples of unacceptable behaviors and the necessary steps to performance improvement. Unlike most of the questions in this section, this one came straight out of the book.

32. C - Prince #3 says that to contribute to the overall business strategy and value creation, HR must be aligned with the entire organizational plan. In order for HR to effectively align itself with organizational strategy, it must present top management with solutions that address the strategic needs of the business. This includes aligning human assets with the business needs.

33. D - Kaplan and Norton theorize that learning and growth (Prince #5) initiatives lead to better business processes (operations cost), which in turn lead to increased value for the customer, which finally leads to improved financial performance, value creation and HR alignment (Prince #3 & #4). Training, productivity and turnover are all measures for the learning perspective.

34. D - Prince #4 (critical thinking) finds the company has three possible answer options to a situation such as this: accept, deny, or stall while seeking clarification. Referring the Attorney to in-house counsel must occur at some point, the better "initial" response is to clarify the issue with an investigation as to the facts (conduct the needs analysis - Prince #1), then respond.

35. A - Application of Prince #4, critical thinking, is needed here. What would you do in real life if you were hit out of the blue with a bombshell like this? First step (Prince #1 - needs analysis), find out as much as you can about the situation. Start investigating before you turn the matter over to counsel (if you have one), informing management, or taking action against the accused. In time, you may answer the Attorney's letter, but in the beginning you do not have enough facts to construct a knowledgeable response.

36. C - Many scenario questions on the HR certification exam give as one of the options, "follow company guidelines." Choose it! Almost every time (got to do a little evaluative thinking, Prince #4, to ensure it is not a red herring answer option)! Company policies are established as an organizational framework to direct appropriate responses to situations such as this. Besides, if it doesn't go well, you can blame the policy... unless you wrote it.